THE TRUE-OR-FALSE BOOK C

HORSE

Patricia Lauber

ILLUSTRATED BY Rosalyn Schanzer

SCHOLASTIC INC.

New York Toronto London Auckland Sydney
Mexico City New Delhi Hong Kong

To Tilly and Buster,
two memorable horses
—*P.L.*

For Adam
and Kim
—*R.S.*

ISBN 0-439-27430-3

12   6/0

Printed in the U.S.A.   40

First Scholastic printing, February 2001

CONTENTS

~

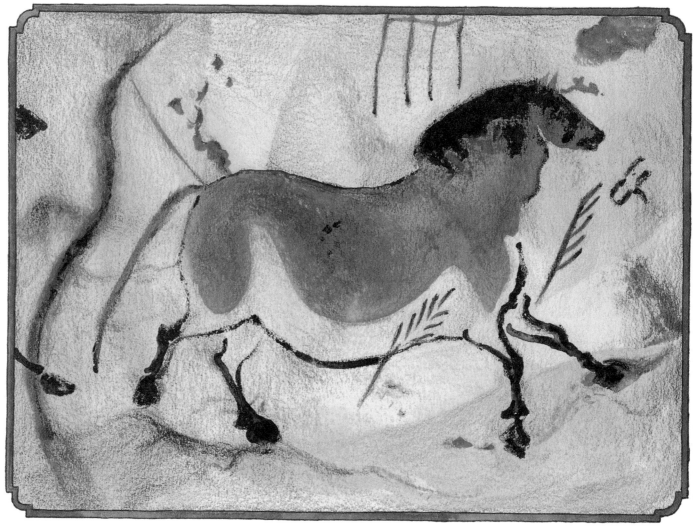

Drawing based on Stone Age art from Lascaux cave in southwestern France

HORSES AND PEOPLE

Some 30,000 years ago, people were painting pictures of horses on the walls of caves. The painters were Stone Age people who lived in what is now Europe. The horses they knew were small, stocky animals, about the size of ponies. The paintings tell us that horses were important to Stone Age people. But they do not tell us if these people learned to herd or tame horses.

We do know that 6,000 years ago people in eastern Europe began taming wild horses of the grasslands. How this happened no one is sure. Perhaps some children wanted a pet, raised a motherless foal, and became the first humans to ride a horse. Whatever happened, the idea of taming horses soon spread.

Once tamed, horses changed human history.

With horses, people could travel farther and faster than on foot. They could take along heavy supplies.

Warfare changed, as warriors on horseback or in chariots swept down on warriors without horses.

People bred different types of horses. Big, sturdy horses worked farmers' fields. Long-legged, lighter horses were prized as racers and hunters.

Not everyone could afford to buy and feed a horse. Most people got about by walking. But for nearly 6,000 years, horses were the chief means of transportation, carrying riders and drawing everything from farmers' wagons to royal coaches.

Then, in the early 1800s, times began to change. The first railroads were built. By the late 1800s, the first automobiles were on the road. Horses were still widely used, but machines were taking their place. Today much of the work once done by horses is done by planes, trains, buses, automobiles, tractors, trucks, and tanks.

Some work on ranches and small farms is still done best by horses. But the horse of today is most likely to be ridden for pleasure or for sport. It is treasured as a handsome, graceful, brave animal—and one that likes people.

Read on and find out how much you know about our friend the horse.

HORSES WALK ON TIPTOE

TRUE OR FALSE?

Horses are big animals. Listen to one *clip-clopping* along a paved road or thumping over a field. It certainly doesn't seem to be traveling on tiptoe. But it really is. Each foot ends in one very long toe. A horse stands, walks, trots, canters, and gallops on the tips of four toes. A horse's foot reaches about halfway up its leg. What looks like a knee to us is really the ankle.

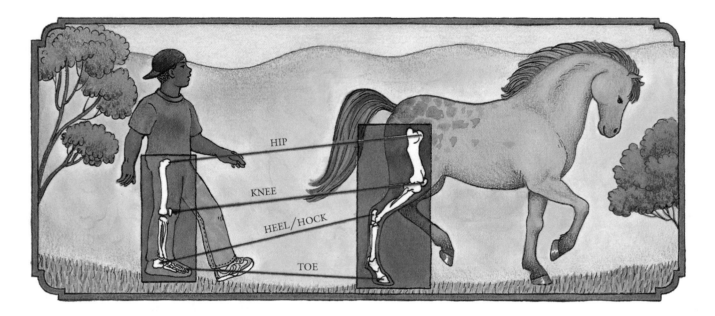

HIP

KNEE

HEEL/HOCK

TOE

Each toe is covered by a hoof made of hard, hornlike material that grows, just as our fingernails do. The outside wall of a hoof is strong enough to support most of a horse's weight.

Paved roads and other hard surfaces can injure hooves. That is why owners shoe their horses with a rim of metal that protects the hoof. Nailing a shoe to the hoof wall does not hurt any more than cutting a fingernail does.

Horses are the fastest land animals
True or false?

With their long legs and strong muscles, horses are fast runners. But the fastest runners of all are cheetahs, or hunting leopards. When a cheetah puts on a burst of speed, it can travel at 60 miles an hour. It can keep up this speed for only a short time—about 15 seconds—but no other land animal can run as fast.

The fastest horses are racehorses. Some can reach a speed of about 40 miles an hour for distances of less than a mile. (The top speed for human runners is about 26 miles an hour for short distances and 15 miles an hour for a mile.)

Horses are excellent at covering long distances quickly. Some have traveled 50 miles in a little more than four hours.

A FAST-TROTTING HORSE SOMETIMES HAS ALL FOUR FEET OFF THE GROUND AT ONE TIME

TRUE OR FALSE?

Watch a trotting horse. You will find you cannot keep track of all four feet at one time. They move too quickly for human eyes to follow. And so for several thousand years, people argued about what a trotting horse did with its feet.

The answer was found in 1877 by an American photographer named Eadweard Muybridge. In those days there were no motion-picture cameras. Muybridge arranged 24 still cameras so that each would be triggered as a trotting horse passed. The photographs showed that at racing speed all four feet do sometimes come off the ground.

FAST TROT

All four feet also come off the ground when a horse canters or gallops. The feet are gathered under the horse. They are not stretched ahead and behind, the way artists used to show them.

CANTER

GALLOP

EARLY EXPLORERS OF THE NEW WORLD WERE GREETED BY INDIANS ON HORSEBACK

TRUE OR FALSE?

About 10,000 years ago, many kinds of animals died out in North America. Among them were horses. What happened is a great mystery. Horses, and their ancestors, had lived in North America for some 55 million years. During that time they had survived many big changes of climate. Then they died out, although other grass eaters, such as bison, did not.

Horses almost died out in the Old World too. But before they did, humans learned to tame and to ride them. Horses were so useful that people began to raise them. Thanks to humans, Old World horses made a comeback.

Horses returned to the New World with explorers. When those early explorers arrived, the Indians were not on horseback. In fact, none of them had ever seen a horse before. Some thought these strange animals must be big dogs.

A HORSE'S TEETH ARE CLUES TO ITS AGE

TRUE OR FALSE?

Horses graze on grass. Grass feels soft underfoot, but it is a tough, coarse food. It is also likely to be gritty with dirt.

A horse uses its lips and front teeth to pull and cut grass. The tongue moves food to the back teeth, which grind it up. Over time, grass and grit wear down a horse's teeth. That is why teeth are a good clue to the age of a horse.

Like a human baby, a foal has milk teeth. It begins to shed these around age two and a half. It grows big, strong adult teeth.

An adult horse has 12 front teeth, or incisors. They are cutting teeth, which look like curved chisels. Each has a pocket, or cup, on the cutting surface. Cups wear away as a horse grows older.

A person who knows what to look for can tell a horse's age by the incisors: Are they milk teeth, adult teeth, or some of each? How much wear do the cups show?

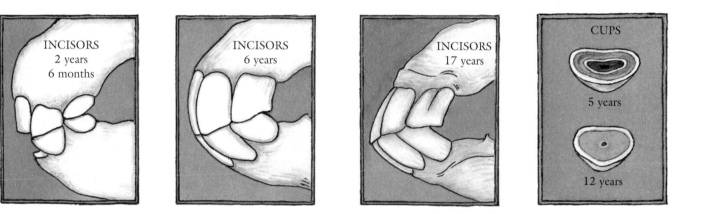

A horse has 24 back teeth, or molars. These grinding teeth are shaped like high columns. As the tops wear off, the teeth keep moving out of the jaw—the upper ones move down, the lower ones up. In a very old horse, these teeth are worn down to the roots.

Horses usually live 20 to 25 years. But a few live to be 30 or 35 or even older.

SKULL WITH INCISORS AND MOLARS

THERE ARE FEW, IF ANY, TRUE WILD HORSES TODAY

TRUE OR FALSE?

There are places, such as the American West, where bands of horses live in the wild. They are often spoken of as "wild horses." But they are not true wild animals. A true wild animal is one that has always lived wild and has only wild ancestors. Most of these horses are descended from domestic horses that escaped from their owners years ago. A few are themselves domestic horses that escaped.

Nikolai Przewalski

There is a special name for animals that live wild but have domestic ancestors. They are called feral. All American horses that live in the wild are feral horses. In the West, they are often called mustangs, from the Spanish word *mesteño*, meaning "strayed" or "wild."

In the 1800s, a Russian explorer discovered some true wild horses in Mongolia. They were named after him—Przewalski's horse. Each was about the size of a large pony, had a short, erect mane, and a flowing tail. These horses looked just like the ones shown in Stone Age cave paintings.

Przewalski's horse can still be seen in zoos and other places where it is being raised. But no one is sure whether such horses still exist in the wild. They may have died out or been hunted to death. Or they may have bred with feral horses of Mongolia. If they do still exist, there can be only a few of these true wild horses.

HORSES CAN SEE IN BACK OF THEMSELVES WITHOUT TURNING THEIR HEADS

TRUE OR FALSE?

A horse has big, bulging eyes, set high and wide on its head. The eyes can see nearly all the way around the horse. A horse does not need to turn its head to see what's behind it. Even when grazing, with its head near the ground, a horse can see around itself far into the distance.

A horse has two blind spots. One is just behind the tail. The other is just in front of the nose. Because of the blind spots, you should always approach a horse from slightly to one side, where it can see you. It is likely to be badly startled if touched or petted by something it can't see.

Horses are also startled by sudden movements. A paper cup blowing along a road may cause a horse to shy or run. Usually a horse's sight is not sharp. It cannot see the cup clearly—it sees only that something is moving. The movement hints of danger, and the horse may act quickly.

HORSES SENSE SMELLS BETTER THAN WE DO

TRUE OR FALSE?

Horses have a keen sense of smell. They can pick up scents that we do not smell at all. In the wild, horses can scent a faraway water hole. They can scent a meat-eating animal that is trying to stalk them. From half a mile away, a stallion can scent a mare that is ready to mate. Mares use their sense of smell to find their own foals.

Sometimes a horse becomes separated from its herd. It can find the others by picking up their scent from the ground and following it.

When two horses meet for the first time, they also use their noses. They sniff each other over carefully. Each smells the other's breath. First one horse blows into the other's nostrils. Then the other horse blows back. From then on, they know each other by smell.

Horses hear sounds that we can't hear

True or false?

A horse has big outer ears that collect sound waves from the air. The ears can be turned separately—one may face forward while the other faces back. A horse easily hears sounds coming from any direction.

A horse can also sense sound waves traveling through the ground. It can hear another horse moving from a quarter of a mile away.

Horses hear many sounds that we can't—sounds that are either too low-pitched or too high-pitched for our ears. They hear distant noises before human riders do. They hear storms that are far away. And horses become nervous and upset shortly before an earthquake strikes. They may well be sensing sounds from deep inside the earth—sounds too low for human ears to hear.

Horses sleep for hours at a time

True or false?

Different animals need different amounts of sleep. Cats sleep or catnap about 16 hours a day. Most humans need around eight hours of sleep. Horses sleep about three hours out of every 24. Some 45 minutes of that time is deep sleep, but it is not a time of solid sleep. A horse sleeps deeply for only about five minutes at a time. Light sleep is also broken into short snoozes. Some of the time a horse is drowsy but still awake.

Lying down and getting up is hard for big animals. A horse must lie down to sleep soundly, but it is able to doze while standing up. Joints in its front and back legs lock together. Because its front and back legs can lock in place, the horse does not need to use its muscles and energy to stay upright. It can rest its body and doze while standing.

SOME HORSES CAN SOLVE MATH PROBLEMS

TRUE OR FALSE?

There was once a horse named Clever Hans, who lived in Germany during the early 1900s. Hans seemed able to do math. Asked to divide 90 by 15, he would paw the ground six times with his right front foot. Hans was rewarded with a sugar cube.

Hans belonged to an elderly schoolmaster, who truly believed he had taught Hans many things. Still, it was hard for others to believe that a horse could do math or tell time.

Finally some scientists found out what was happening. Horses are good learners and have excellent memories. They

are also quick to sense what people are feeling. Without meaning to, the master was tensing up as Hans started to paw the ground. When Hans reached the right number, the master relaxed. Hans had learned that if he stopped pawing when his master relaxed, he was given a sugar cube.

The scientists showed that Hans could solve a problem only if someone near him knew the answer. Asked out loud to add two and five, Hans would paw the ground seven times. But if one person whispered to Hans, "Add two," and another person whispered, "And five," then no person knew the answer—and Hans didn't know when to stop pawing. There was no cue for him to pick up.

Other horses have seemed able to do math, answer questions, and even read minds. But it has always turned out that the horses were picking up cues from humans.

HORSES MAKE MANY KINDS OF SOUNDS THAT SERVE AS MESSAGES

TRUE OR FALSE?

Many animals make a wide variety of sounds—cats, dogs, birds, and monkeys are four that do. Horses make only a few sounds. Sometimes you hear a horse groan if it is working hard. It may sigh. It may snore loudly. But these sounds do not carry messages. There are five sounds that do.

The *nicker* is a soft, gentle, low sound. It is often a greeting to a friend—another horse or a human. Mares nicker when calling their foals.

The *snort* is made when a horse blows a rapid pulse of air through its nose. This is a loud, fluttering noise that warns of possible danger, such as a strange object seen in the distance. The snort clears the horse's nose and windpipe for action. A snorting horse is excited and ready to flee if it must.

The *blow* is much like the snort but without the flutter. The horse may be wondering about what it sees, but it is not alarmed. Sometimes a horse blows just because it is feeling good.

The *squeal* is much louder and higher than the snort. Some of the loudest squeals are heard when two stallions meet and face off. Their squeals may take the place of a fight—the one that squeals longest wins.

The *whinny*, or *neigh*, is the loudest sound a horse makes. It starts as high as a squeal and ends as low as a nicker. It can be heard half a mile away. A horse whinnies to keep in touch with other horses that are out of sight. Horses seem to recognize one another by their whinnies. A foal knows its mother's whinny and the mother knows her foal's.

27

ONE WAY TO TELL HOW A HORSE IS FEELING IS TO LOOK AT ITS BODY

TRUE OR FALSE?

Feral horses live on open grasslands, where members of a herd are usually in sight of one another. Each can read another horse's mood by looking at its body. Domestic horses use the same signals, and we can read them if we know how.

A swishing tail shows that a horse is out of sorts. It may be trying to get rid of a fly that is pestering it. Or it may be cross for some other reason. A swishing tail is a warning to keep away.

Laid-back ears are another warning. A horse with laid-back ears is prepared to fight.

A cocked ear shows interest in a sound.

Pawing with a front foot often shows impatience.

A lifted back leg signals that a kick is on the way.

A horse that swings its head, with mouth open and teeth bared, is threatening to bite.

When a horse is excited or interested, its whole body seems to grow taller. The head is held high and the tail stands up. When a horse is sleepy or bored, its head, tail, and body slump.

Horses rarely fight one another. The reason seems to be that threats keep the peace. When one horse backs off, there is no need to fight over food, water, or mates.

HORSES ARE SOCIAL ANIMALS— THEY ENJOY COMPANY

TRUE OR FALSE?

Feral horses live in small bands—a stallion, his mares, and their young foals. The members of a band recognize one another by sight and smell and sound. They develop tight bonds of friendship. Horses are social animals that enjoy company. They like the company of other horses best. Without it, domestic horses seek the company of humans— or the barn cat.

Two horses show their friendship by grooming each other. Each horse nibbles the other's mane, neck, shoulders, and back. These are all areas that are hard for a horse to groom by itself. Grooming is pleasurable and calming—a horse's heart rate slows when it is being groomed.

If you are a rider, it's a good idea to curry and brush your own horse. Grooming shows that you want to be friends. You may even be rewarded with a kind of kiss—the brush of a velvety muzzle against your cheek.